1–PAGE MARKETING PLAN GUIDE BOOK

draw in New customers boost your income and outshine your competitors

BRYAN M. GROVER

Introduction:

There once was a young woman named Sarah who had long imagined opening her bakery. She had a love for baking and enjoyed nothing more than making delectable galettes and desserts for her family and musketeers. Nevertheless, Sarah had no idea how to go about beginning a firm. She had never attended any business classes and had no idea how to develop a marketing strategy or a business plan. Sarah came upon a book on beginning a small business one day while perusing a genuine bookstore. She decided to read it out of curiosity. The book included detailed instructions on everything from developing a company plan to using marketing techniques. Sarah took in the knowledge and learned. She spent months refining her clothing lines, branding her company, and building a website. She advertised her bakery on social media and did provide free samples to unique businesses. The book's advice helped Sarah's Bakery swiftly build a following. Her galettes and afters were a smashing success, and visitors praised her for her meticulous attention to detail and attentive service. As her company expanded, Sarah continued to relate to the book by maintaining her focus on her aspirations and adhering to her plans as necessary. She gained new skills in managing her finances, creating powerful marketing campaigns, and building trusting relationships with her visitors. Sarah's bakery is currently a booming business. She has grown her company to offer catering services. and has created a substitute post. She has earned the respect of the original business community thanks to the great demand for her galettes and afters. Sarah says that the book gave her the information and self-assurance she needed to turn her ambition into a reality. Without it, she might not have had the guts to start her own business or take the first step. Finally, Sarah's experience serves as a tribute to the strength of education and willpower. Anyone can establish a successful business and realize their aspirations with the correct help and direction. There is a book available that can assist you in beginning your journey to success, regardless of whether you are a chef, a writer, or an entrepreneur in any other sector.

In today's fast-paced business world, it's essential to have a well-planned and executed marketing strategy to stay ahead of the competition.

However, many businesses struggle to create an effective marketing plan that delivers results. That's where the one page marketing guide book comes in. This comprehensive approach to marketing provides a step-by-step guide to creating a successful marketing campaign. From identifying your target audience to creating compelling content and measuring your results, the one page marketing guide covers all the essential elements of a successful marketing strategy. In this article, we'll explore the benefits of the one page marketing guide and provide tips on how to create a winning marketing campaign.

Chapter 1: The Foundation of Your 1-page Marketing guide book

A 1-page marketing guide book requires a solid foundation to insure its effectiveness and success. This comprehensive companion will walk you through the essential rudiments that form the base of a 1-page marketing guide book, setting you up for a focused and poignant marketing campaign within a short period. Define Clear and Measurable pretensions by defining clear and specific marketing pretensions for your 1-page marketing guide book. These pretensions should be measurable and aligned with your overall business objects. examples may include adding website business by a certain chance, generating a specific number of leads, or achieving a set number of deals transformations. Identify Your Target followership Understanding your target followership is pivotal for effective marketing. Identify your ideal client profile and produce detailed buyer personas. Consider demographic information, preferences, pain points, and geste

patterns. This knowledge will help you conform your marketing dispatches and choose the most suitable marketing modalities. Perform competitor analysis Analyze your competitors to discover their virtues, flaws, and marketing tactics. Find out what makes your company unique and how you can set yourself apart. This investigation will provide priceless insight that can guide your marketing strategy and assist you in strategically placing your immolations.   Make a SWOT analysis. To evaluate your business or design, conduct a thorough geek analysis (Strengths, flaws, Openings, and Pitfalls). evaluate the request's external openings and perils as well as your own virtues and transgressions. You can use this study to better understand your competitive advantage and the underlying issues that your 1-page marketing plan has to address. Choose the Right Marketing Channels select the most applicable marketing channels grounded on your target audience and pretensions. Consider options similar to social media platforms, dispatch marketing, content marketing, paid advertising, hunt machine optimization(SEO), influencer marketing, or offline strategies like events or hookups. Choose channels that align with your audience's preferences and give the stylish occasion to achieve your objects within the one- week timeframe. Craft Compelling crucial dispatches Develop crucial dispatches that effectively communicate your value proposition and reverberate with your target audience. ensure your dispatches are clear, terse, and align with your brand's tone and values. Craft compelling captions, taglines, and elevator pitches that snare attention and produce a continuing impact. producing Engaging Content, Content plays a pivotal part in any marketing plan. produce high- quality content that educates, entertains, or inspires your target followership. This can include blog posts, social media content, videos, infographics, or dispatch newsletters. conform your content to address your audiences pain points and give results while aligning with your overall marketing pretensions. Develop a Content timetable Organize your content creation and distribution by creating a content timetable. Chart out the motifs, formats, and distribution schedule for each piece of content. This will help you maintain a harmonious inflow of communication throughout the week and ensure timely prosecution of your marketing plan. Set a Realistic Budget Allocate a budget for your 1-page marketing plan to determine the coffers you can devote to colorful marketing conditioning. Consider both paid and organic strategies and allocate your budget strategically to maximize your impact within the given timeframe. Establish crucial Performance pointers(KPIs) Identify crucial performance pointers(KPIs) to measure the success of your marketing sweats. These may include website business, conversion rates, engagement criteria , supereminent generation, or deals numbers. Set specific targets for each KPI to track your progress and estimate the effectiveness of your one- week marketing plan.

Examiner and Optimize in Real- Time Throughout the short period marketing plan, nearly cover your juggernauts and acclimate your strategies grounded on real- time data and perceptivity. use analytics tools, social media perceptivity, and other applicable criteria to assess performance.

Defining Your Target Market

Characterizing your objective market is a basic move toward fostering a fruitful business or promoting technique. It includes distinguishing and understanding the particular gathering of clients or clients that your items or administrations are expected for. By characterizing your objective market, you can tailor your contributions, informing, and promoting endeavors to reach and connect with the right crowd actually. Here are a vital stages to assist you with

characterizing your objective market:
Research and examine your item or **administration:** Begin by completely grasping the highlights, advantages, and interesting selling points of your item or administration.

This will assist you with recognizing the particular requirements, issues, or wants it satisfies for clients.

Fragment your market:
Break down the bigger market into more modest sections in light of important qualities like socioeconomics (age, orientation, pay, schooling), psychographics (way of life, interests, values), conduct (purchasing behaviors, item utilization), or geographic area. For instance, on the off chance that you sell wellness attire, your objective market sections could incorporate dynamic experts, wellness aficionados, or competitors.

Assess market appeal:

Evaluate each market section's size, development potential, rivalry, and benefit.
Figure out which portions adjust best to your business objectives, assets, and capacities.

Characterize your optimal client persona:
Make a point by point profile of your ideal client in view of the distinguished market segment(s). Incorporate factors, for example, age, orientation, occupation, side interests, inclinations, trouble spots, and inspirations. This persona ought to address your objective market's qualities and act as a source of perspective point for navigation.
Lead statistical surveying: Assemble information through overviews, interviews, center gatherings, or online exploration to approve your

suppositions and gain bits of knowledge into your objective market's way of behaving, inclinations, and purchasing propensities. Utilize both quantitative and subjective strategies to assemble a balanced comprehension.

Break down rivalry: Study your rivals who take special care of comparable objective business sectors. Distinguish their assets, shortcomings, and holes in the market that you can use. Separate your contributions by distinguishing what separates you and why clients ought to pick your business over others.

Refine and focus on: In light of the examination and examination, thin down your objective market to the most encouraging sections that line up with your business goals and have the most noteworthy potential for progress.

Center your assets and endeavors around those sections at first, and extend later as your business develops.

Test and emphasize: Carry out designated advertising efforts or experimental runs projects to test your presumptions and assemble criticism. Screen the outcomes and be available to change your objective market definition in view of new experiences or changing business sector elements.

Recollect that characterizing your objective market is a continuous interaction. As your business advances and economic situations change, consistently reevaluate and refine how you might interpret your objective market to successfully remain pertinent and address your clients' issues

Identifying Your Unique Selling Proposition

Distinguishing your One of a kind Selling Recommendation (USP) is fundamental for laying out an upper hand on the lookout and drawing in clients. Your USP is the unmistakable variable that sets your item, administration, or brand separated from contenders and persuades clients to pick you over others. Here are a few central issues to consider while recognizing your USP:

Comprehend your objective market: Begin by acquiring a profound comprehension of your interest group's necessities, inclinations, and trouble spots.

This information will assist you with fitting your USP to address their particular difficulties and wants.

Examine your opposition: Lead an exhaustive examination of your rivals to distinguish holes on the lookout and regions where you can separate yourself. Search for valuable chances to offer something one of a kind or to succeed in a specific perspective that your rivals are ignoring.

Center around your assets: Distinguish your key assets, whether it's predominant item quality, outstanding client support, imaginative elements, or a particular specialty. Influence these qualities to make a convincing USP that reverberates with your objective market.

Underscore benefits: Obviously impart the advantages that clients will insight by picking your item or administration. Feature how your contribution tackles their concerns, sets aside time or cash, works on their lives, or gives a special encounter.

Test and refine: Whenever you have figured out your USP, test it with your interest group to check their reaction. Look for input and make changes depending on the situation to guarantee that your USP actually catches their consideration and persuades them to pick you.

Laying out clear and distinct showcasing objectives is vital for the progress of any business. These objectives act as a guide, directing your showcasing endeavors and giving an internal compass.

They assist you with centering your assets, measure progress, and assess the viability of your promoting techniques. The following are a couple of central issues to consider while laying out your promoting objectives.

Right off the bat, your objectives ought to be explicit and quantifiable. Unclear objectives like "increment deals" or "further develop brand mindfulness" are not significant. All things being equal, set explicit targets like "increment deals by 20% in the following quarter" or "create 1,000 new leads each month." This permits you to follow headway and make changes depending on the situation.

Also, your objectives ought to be sensible and achievable. While it's essential to reach skyward, laying out unreachable objectives can prompt dissatisfaction and demotivation.

Consider factors, for example, your industry, economic situations, accessible assets, and verifiable information while defining your objectives.

Moreover, your objectives ought to be time-bound. Set a cutoff time or time span for accomplishing every objective. This adds a need to keep moving and assists you with focusing on undertakings and distribute assets successfully.

Finally, adjust your showcasing objectives to your general business targets. Your showcasing endeavors ought to add to the bigger objectives of your association, whether it's raising a piece of the pie, venturing into new business sectors, or sending off new items.

Make sure to routinely audit and change your advertising objectives depending on the situation. Economic situations and business needs can change, and it's vital to remain spry and receptive to these changes. By laying out clear advertising objectives, you can concentrate your endeavors, measure achievement, and drive your business forward

Chapter 2: The Marketing Mix

The showcasing blend, otherwise called the 4Ps of promoting, is a crucial structure that guides organizations in creating and executing successful promoting systems. It comprises four key components: item, value, spot, and advancement. Every part assumes an essential part in molding an organization's promoting approach and accomplishing its goals.

The principal component, item, alludes to the labor and products an organization offers to fulfill client needs. It includes viewpoints, for example, item configuration, highlights, quality, bundling, and marking. Understanding the objective market's inclinations and requests is fundamental for fostering a convincing item that separates itself from contenders and makes an incentive for clients.

Value alludes to the financial worth doled out to an item or administration. Setting the right cost is basic as it straightforwardly influences an organization's income and productivity. Factors like creation costs, contender evaluating, client view of significant worth, and estimating procedures, for example, infiltration valuing or skimming estimating, should be considered to decide on an ideal evaluating system.

Place alludes to the circulation channels and where clients can get to the item. It includes choices connected with stock administration, warehousing, transportation, and retail or online presence.

A successful spot methodology guarantees that the item is accessible with flawless timing and spot, making it advantageous for clients to buy.

Advancement includes the different showcasing exercises used to impart and elevate the item to the objective market. It incorporates promoting, advertising, deals advancements, direct showcasing, and computerized showcasing endeavors. The objective is to make mindfulness, create interest, and convince clients to pick the item over contenders. A very much-planned advancement technique considers the interest group, the best correspondence channels, and the ideal message to accomplish the greatest effect.

While the 4Ps structure gives a strong groundwork to showcasing procedures, it is vital to take note that the promoting blend ought to be adjusted and redone because of the novel qualities of every business and its objective market. Moreover, as of late, extra components like individuals, process, and actual proof have been included, particularly in help-based enterprises, to more readily address client experience and administration conveyance.

All in all, the showcasing blend is an extensive system that assists organizations with settling on informed conclusions about their item, value, spot, and advancement methodologies. Via cautiously considering every component and its effect on consumer loyalty and the upper hand, organizations can foster compelling promoting efforts that address client issues, drive deals, and at last make business progress

Understanding the Four Ps of Marketing

Grasping the Four Ps of Advertising

The Four Ps of showcasing, otherwise called the promoting blend, is a basic structure that assists organizations with creating successful advertising methodologies. These four components, in particular Item, Value, Spot, and Advancement, give a thorough comprehension of how to situate an item or administration on the lookout and draw in target clients. How about we dive further into every one of these parts and their importance in showcasing?

Item: The item is the center contribution of an organization, whether it's an actual item or an immaterial help.

It includes the elements, advantages, and special selling suggestions (USP) that separate it from contenders. Understanding the objective market's necessities and inclinations is vital for fostering an item that meets their prerequisites and makes esteem. This includes directing statistical surveying, examining client criticism, and consistently working on the item to remain pertinent in a powerful market.

Value: Evaluating is an essential choice that straightforwardly influences an organization's income and benefit. Setting the right cost includes considering elements, for example, creation costs, contest, client discernment, and market interest. Organizations can take on different estimating methodologies, for example, cost-based evaluating, esteem-based valuing, or entrance evaluating, contingent upon their goals. The picked estimating procedure ought to line up with the apparent worth of the item and the objective market's ability to pay.

Place: Spot alludes to the conveyance channels through which items or administrations arrive at clients. It includes deciding the best method for making the item accessible and available to the objective market. This could incorporate direct deals through organization-claimed stores, online stages, outsider retailers, or a blend of these channels. The objective is to guarantee the item is strategically placed where clients are probably going to search for it, giving simplicity of procurement and ideal conveyance.

Advancement: Advancement incorporates every one of the exercises organizations attempt to convey and advance their item or administration to the interest group. This incorporates publicizing, advertising, deals advancements, direct promoting, and computerized showcasing endeavors. Viable advancement systems consider the objective market's inclinations, ways of behaving, and media utilization propensities. By making convincing showcasing messages and choosing the right correspondence channels, organizations can reach and impact their clients.

It's essential to take note that the Four Ps are interrelated and ought to be viewed together while creating advertising systems. Changes in a single component can affect the others. For instance, a top-notch estimating procedure could require a comparing accentuation on item quality and better advancement than legitimizing the more exorbitant cost. Thus, a comprehensive methodology is important to guarantee cognizance and consistency across the showcasing blend.

All in all, understanding and using the Four Ps of advertising can assist organizations with creating powerful showcasing techniques. Via cautiously thinking about the item, value, spot, and advancement components, organizations can adjust their contributions to client needs, make an upper hand, and drive business achievement.

Creating a Product Strategy

Coming up with an item procedure is a pivotal move toward the turn of events and outcome of any item. It includes characterizing the objectives, target market, and serious situation of the item to guarantee its feasibility on the lookout. A very much-created item system fills in as a guide for the whole item lifecycle, directing the turn of events, promoting, and circulation endeavors.

To formulate a viable item methodology, a few key advances ought to be followed. It, first and foremost, is vital to lead exhaustive statistical surveying to comprehend client necessities, inclinations, and market patterns.

This examination assists in recognizing the objective with advertising and potential client fragments, permitting the item group to appropriately tailor the system.

Then, characterizing clear objectives and targets is fundamental. These objectives ought to be explicit, quantifiable, reachable, pertinent, and time-bound (Shrewd). They act as the establishment for the item technique and assist with adjusting the group towards a typical vision.

Besides, cutthroat examination assumes a pivotal part in forming the item system. Grasping the qualities and shortcomings of contenders, as well as recognizing any holes on the lookout, can give important experiences to separation and situating.

When the preparation is laid, essential to foster an incentive conveys the remarkable offering focuses and advantages of the item to clients. This incentive ought to address the trouble spots of the objective market and show how the item takes care of their concerns or satisfies their necessities better than choices.

Ultimately, the item procedure ought to frame the key highlights, evaluation, dissemination channels, and advertising approach for the item. It ought to likewise incorporate a course of events and financial plan to guarantee powerful execution.

All in all, thinking up an item technique is a basic cycle that requires cautious exploration, objective setting, cutthroat examination, and offers a turn of events.

A very much-created item system sets the heading for the item's turn of events and guides its effective send-off and showcase infiltration.

Developing a Pricing Strategy

Fostering a valuing technique is an essential part of any business, as it straightforwardly influences benefit, market situating, and client discernment. A very planned evaluation methodology thinks about different variables, for example, costs, rivalry, client worth, and market elements, to decide the ideal cost for an item or administration.

The most vital phase in fostering a valuing procedure is to comprehend the costs engaged with creating and conveying the item or administration.

This incorporates both direct expenses, like materials and work, as well as circuitous costs like the above costs. By precisely surveying these expenses, a business can lay out a gauge for estimating that guarantees benefit.

Then, assessing the cutthroat landscape is fundamental. Understanding how comparative items or administrations are evaluated by contenders gives experience in market assumptions and situating. A business can decide to separate itself through valuing, whether by offering an exceptional item at a greater cost or by giving a more reasonable choice to draw in cost delicate clients.

Client esteem is one more basic component to consider. It includes understanding the apparent advantages and worth that clients get from the item or administration.

An evaluating technique ought to line up with the incentive of the contribution, guaranteeing that clients feel they are getting a fair incentive for their speculation.

Market elements, for example, request flexibility and market patterns, ought to likewise be considered. Valuing systems can be changed in light of interest variances, occasional examples, or changes in client inclinations to boost deals and income.

At long last, an estimating system ought to be versatile and adaptable. Standard observing and investigation of valuing execution, client criticism, and economic situations take into consideration changes and refinements over the long haul.

All in all, fostering an estimating system requires cautious thought of expenses, contest, client worth, and market elements. By finding the right harmony between these variables, organizations can set costs that drive productivity, draw in clients, and lay out areas of strength for a position.

Crafting a Promotion Strategy

Creating an Advancement System

A very much-planned advancement technique is fundamental for organizations trying to increment brand mindfulness, draw in new clients, and eventually drive deals. With a painstakingly arranged approach, organizations can convey their incentive, separate themselves from contenders, and draw in their interest groups. Here are critical stages to consider while making an advancement methodology.

Characterize targets: Start by explaining the particular objectives you intend to accomplish through your advancement endeavors. Is it true that you are hoping to increment deals, send off another item, or improve memorability? Laying out clear goals will direct your procedure and assist you with deciding the most proper limited-time strategies.

Know your interest group: Understanding your interest group is significant for making a fruitful advancement methodology. Distinguish their socioeconomics, inclinations, ways of behaving, and correspondence channels regularly. This information will empower you to tailor your information and select the best limited-time stages.

Foster a convincing message: Specialty is a convincing and succinct message that passes on your extraordinary offer and resounds with your interest group. Feature the advantages your item or administration offers and address any problem areas your clients might have. Underscore what separates you from contenders to make areas of strength for a character.

Pick the right special channels: Consider the best channels to arrive at your interest group. This could incorporate advanced stages like virtual entertainment, email promoting, site design improvement, or conventional strategies like print advertisements, TV, radio, or regular postal mail.

Each channel has its assets and shortcomings, so select those that line up with your goals and ideal interest group.

Use a blend of strategies: A fruitful advancement system frequently consolidates different strategies to expand reach and commitment. This might incorporate running web-based publicizing efforts, offering limits or impetuses, making enlightening and drawing in happy, facilitating occasions or online classes, or banding together with powerhouses or different brands for co-promoting amazing open doors.

Screen and measure results: Lay out key execution pointers (KPIs) to quantify the adequacy of your advancement system.

Track measurements, for example, site traffic, transformation rates, online entertainment commitment, and deals income.

Break down the information consistently and put forth acclimations to enhance your limited-time attempts. Adjust and refine: The market scene and buyer conduct are continually advancing, so it's significant to remain light-footed and adjust your advancement technique as needs be. Constantly assess the outcomes, gather client input, and remain refreshed on industry patterns. Be ready to refine your way to deal with guarantee continuous achievement.

All in all, creating an advancement methodology requires an extensive comprehension of your goals, main interest group, information, and limited time channels.

By following these means and consistently checking and refining your endeavors, you can foster an advancement system that successfully imparts your image's worth, connects with your crowd, and drives wanted results.

Implementing a Place (Distribution) Strategy

Carrying out a Spot (Dissemination) Methodology

A clear-cut dissemination methodology is pivotal for the progress of any business. It includes the most common way of getting items or administrations from the maker to the end shopper productively and really. This cycle, known as spot or conveyance, envelops different exercises like transportation, warehousing, stock administration, and channel choice.

Carrying out a vigorous spot methodology requires cautious preparation and thought of a few key elements. Here are some significant stages to consider:

Comprehend client needs: The most important phase in fostering a circulation system is to comprehend the requirements and inclinations of your objective clients completely. This incorporates their topographical area, purchasing conduct, and assumptions about item accessibility and conveyance. By acquiring bits of knowledge about your clients' necessities, you can plan a dissemination network that satisfies their needs.

Select circulation channels: Contingent upon your item and target market, you want to decide the most fitting dissemination channels to arrive at your clients. These channels can incorporate direct deals, wholesalers, retailers, internet business stages, or a mix of various channels. Each channel enjoys its benefits and difficulties, so it's fundamental to assess them in light of variables like expense, control, reach, and client experience.

Construct solid associations with mediators: On the off chance that your appropriation procedure includes working with delegates, for example, wholesalers or retailers, laying major areas of strength out with them is essential. Team up intimately with your middle people, furnish them with essential preparation and backing, and proposition motivating forces to energize their dynamic cooperation in advancing and selling your items.

By cultivating solid organizations, you can guarantee a smooth progression of merchandise from your creation offices to the end purchasers.

Upgrade stock administration: Effective stock administration is basic to keep away from stockouts and overabundance of stock.

By carrying out stock control frameworks and utilizing advances like in the nick of time (JIT) or merchant oversaw stock (VMI), you can smooth out the development of items through the production network. This guarantees that you have the perfect proportion of stock at the ideal locations and time, limiting conveying costs while fulfilling client needs.

Guarantee consistent strategies: Operations assume an urgent part in fruitful circulation. It includes overseeing transportation, warehousing, and request satisfaction processes. Select solid transportation accomplices or layout in-house operations capacities to guarantee convenient and practical item conveyance. Effective warehousing and request satisfaction frameworks empower you to store, pack, and boat items productively, upgrading consumer loyalty.

Screen and adjust: Executing a conveyance technique is not a one-time process. Consistently screen the presentation of your dispersion channels and make changes on a case-by-case basis.

Track key execution pointers (KPIs, for example, deals volumes, request fill rates, on-time conveyance, and client input. This information will give experiences into regions that require improvement or changes following the technique to upgrade by and large adequacy.

All in all, executing a spot (dissemination) technique requires cautious preparation, understanding client needs, choosing proper conveyance channels, and areas of strength for building with mediators, upgrading stock administration, guaranteeing consistent coordinated factors, and ceaselessly checking and adjusting the methodology.

By really dealing with the appropriation cycle, organizations can arrive at their objective clients effectively, upgrade consumer loyalty, and at last drive development and achievement.

Chapter 3: Creating Your 1-page Marketing Plan

Section 3: Making Your One-page Advertising Plan

In the speedy universe of showcasing, having a distinct and significant arrangement is essential for progress. In Part 3 of "Making Your One-page Showcasing Plan," we dig into the most common way of fostering an extensive promoting methodology that can be executed in a short period. This section gives advertisers the instruments and experiences important to proficiently design, execute, and assess their promoting endeavors.

The section starts by stressing the significance of laying out clear targets and objectives. Without a reasonable bearing, promoting exercises can become dissipated and incapable.

By characterizing explicit, quantifiable, attainable, significant, and time-bound (Shrewd) objectives, advertisers can adjust their endeavors toward accomplishing substantial outcomes. The part gives down-to-earth tips and guides to assist perusers with making Shrewd objectives custom fitted to their particular business needs.

Then, the section plunges into statistical surveying and investigation. Understanding the ideal interest group and the cutthroat scene is principal to fostering a successful showcasing plan. Perusers are acquainted with different examination techniques, for example, client overviews, contender investigation, and market pattern examination, to assemble important experiences. Furnished with this data, advertisers can more readily distinguish their interesting selling recommendations and foster methodologies that resound with their objective market.

The part then, at that point, guides users through the method involved with choosing suitable promoting channels and strategies. With the steadily extending exhibit of showcasing channels accessible, picking the most appropriate ones can overpower. The section gives an outline of conventional and computerized showcasing channels, featuring their assets and impediments. Perusers are urged to use a blend of channels to boost their span and commitment.

Moreover, the section accentuates the significance of making convincing and predictable information across all showcasing materials. Whether it's online entertainment posts, email pamphlets, or site content, keeping a firm brand voice and informing is essential for building trust and unwavering ness with clients.

Ultimately, the part stresses the meaning of following and assessing showcasing endeavors. By setting key execution pointers (KPIs) and observing effort execution, advertisers can distinguish what's working and what needs improvement. The part gives down-to-earth tips on dissecting information and going with information-driven choices to upgrade promoting systems.

All in all, Section 3 of "Making Your One-page Promoting Plan" furnishes advertisers with a deliberate way to deal with fostering a viable showcasing technique in a period-obligated climate. By defining clear objectives, directing intensive statistical surveying, choosing proper channels, creating convincing information, and following execution, advertisers can boost their promoting endeavors and accomplish wanted results soon.

Making a one-page showcasing plan layout can be a significant instrument for organizations hoping to smooth out their promoting endeavors and accomplish their objectives within a short period. A very planned plan can give clearness, concentration, and design, guaranteeing that consistently is used successfully to expand results. Here is a proposed system for building your one-week showcasing plan layout. To begin with, begin by characterizing your goals for the week. Whether it's rising image mindfulness, producing leads, or driving deals, obviously articulating your objectives will act as a core value all through the arranging system.

Then, recognize your ideal interest group and direct a fast investigation of their inclinations, ways of behaving, and needs. This data will assist you with fitting your showcasing messages and selecting the most suitable channels to contact your crowd.

Considering your objectives and crowd, frame explicit showcasing strategies for every day of the week. These could incorporate substance creation, web-based entertainment crusades, email promoting, paid publicizing, or systems administration exercises. Make certain to assign time and assets in like manner, and focus on undertakings given their expected effect.

Consider integrating execution measurements into your arrangement to follow the viability of your advertising exercises.

This could incorporate estimating site traffic, commitment rates, change rates, or client input. Routinely surveying these measurements will permit you to make information-driven acclimations to your arrangement on a case-by-case basis.

Finally, assess and dissect the outcomes toward the week's end. Evaluate the progress of your endeavors against your underlying goals and recognize regions for development. Utilize these experiences to refine your future advertising plans and enhance your general technique.

By building a one-page promoting plan layout, you can effectively deal with your showcasing exercises, keep on track, and accomplish significant outcomes within a more limited period. Make sure to stay adaptable and adjust your arrangement as important to oblige any unforeseen open doors or difficulties that might emerge.

Filling in the Key Sections of Your Plan

While making an arrangement, it is vital to guarantee that all key segments are satisfactorily filled in to give an extensive guide to progress. These key segments act as the underpinning of your arrangement and give an unmistakable bearing to accomplishing your objectives.

The leader synopsis, right off the bat, ought to concisely sum up the whole arrangement, featuring its motivation, targets, and key methodologies.

It fills in as an outline that catches the pursuer's consideration and gives a depiction of the arrangement's items.

Then, the presentation ought to give foundation data, a setting, and an outline of the issue or opportunity the arrangement plans to address. This segment makes way until the end of the arrangement and assists the peruser with grasping the reasoning behind your systems.

The primary body of the arrangement ought to remember point-by-point segments for regions like market examination, main interest group, cutthroat investigation, showcasing and deals methodologies, functional plans, and monetary projections. These segments give a far-reaching comprehension of the market scene, target clients, rivalry, and the means expected to accomplish your goals.

Finally, an end ought, to sum up the arrangement's central issues, emphasize the goals, and give a convincing source of inspiration. It builds up the arrangement's significance and leaves the peruser with a reasonable comprehension of the subsequent stages to be taken.

By perseveringly filling in these key segments, your arrangement turns into a useful asset that directs your activities, works with navigation, and improves the probability of progress.

Tips for Making Your Plan Clear and Concise

Concerning making arrangements, clearness and compactness are critical for viable correspondence and execution. Here are a few hints to assist you with making a reasonable and **compact arrangement:**

Characterize your goal: Begin by plainly expressing the reason and wanted result of your arrangement. This helps center your endeavors and guarantees everybody figures out the ultimate objective.

Utilize straightforward language: Keep away from language and specialized terms that might confound your crowd. Settle direct and effectively reasonable language to convey your thoughts.

Separate it: Gap your arrangement into more modest, reasonable errands or steps. This gives an unmistakable guide and makes it simpler for others to track.

Be explicit: Give exact subtleties and incorporate important data, for example, timetables, assets required, and obligations. Vagueness can prompt mistaken assumptions and prevent progress.

Trim superfluous data: Audit your arrangement and take out any pointless or repetitive subtleties. Keep it compact by including just the fundamental data.

Utilize visual guides: Integrate outlines, charts, or diagrams to represent complex ideas or cycles.

Visuals can improve clearness and make your arrangement seriously captivating.

Keep in mind, a reasonable and compact arrangement guarantees that everybody in question figures out their jobs and obligations, prompting better joint effort and fruitful execution

Chapter 4: Putting Your One-Page Marketing Plan into Action

In Section 4, we dig into the valuable execution of your one-page advertising plan. Furnished with an unmistakable vision and "key" goals illustrated in the past sections, now is the right time to execute your showcasing technique.

The section starts by accentuating" the significance of adjusting your advertising exercises to your ideal interest group. By figuring out their necessities, inclinations, and ways of behaving, you can tailor your information and strategies to reach and connect with them successfully.

Then, we investigate different advertising channels and mediums accessible to advance your item or administration. From customary roads like print and TV to computerized stages, for example, virtual entertainment and email showcasing, each channel has its interesting advantages and contemplations. The section guides you in choosing the most appropriate channels in light of your ideal interest group and spending plan.

Besides, the part features the meaning of reliable marking across all advertising endeavors. By keeping up a durable and unmistakable brand personality, you can fabricate trust and steadfastness among shoppers.

At last, the part stresses the significance of checking and estimating the presentation of your advertising drives. By pursuing key measurements and making information-driven changes, you can enhance your systems for improved results.

Section 4 gives you the functional devices and experiences significant to carry out your one-page advertising plan "certainly" and accomplish your business targets.

Identifying Key Metrics to Track

Distinguishing key measurements to follow is essential for estimating the achievement and progress of any undertaking. Whether it's a business, task, or individual objective, following the "right" measurements gives significant bits of knowledge and empowers informed independent direction. The most important phase in this cycle is "obviously characterizing the goal or wanted result. When the goal is laid out, applicable measurements "can be "distinguished" Key measurements ought to be explicit, quantifiable, and lined up with the objective. For instance, in a "deal" setting, key "measurements" might incorporate all-out income, transformation rate, "normal" request worth, and client procurement cost. These measurements give a complete perspective on the business execution and assist with recognizing regions for development.

Moreover, it's vital to think about the unique situation and period while choosing measurements.

A few measurements might be more significant when followed over a more extended period, while others might call for constant checking.

Constantly checking on and breaking down key measurements takes into account proactive changes and the ID of patterns or examples. It empowers partners to pursue information-driven choices, enhance techniques, and distribute assets successfully. Eventually, distinguishing key measurements to follow is a fundamental stage towards making progress and ceaseless improvement.

Creating an Action Plan for Implementation

Making an activity plan for execution is pivotal to guarantee the effective execution of any venture or drive.

To foster a compelling activity plan, a few key advances should be followed.

To start with, obviously characterize the targets and objectives of the task. This will give an "unmistakable" course to the activity plan and assist with focusing on undertakings.

Then, separate the targets into explicit, quantifiable, feasible, significant, and time-bound (Savvy) errands. Each undertaking ought to have an unmistakable proprietor and cutoff time for the finish.

Recognize the expected assets, like a financial plan, faculty, and materials, and assign them appropriately.

Lay out a timetable with achievements and cutoff times to follow the progress and keep the execution on the target.

Impart the activity plan to all partners "included", guaranteeing everybody figures out their jobs and obligations.

Routinely screen and assess the execution progress to distinguish any difficulties or deviations from the arrangement. Make vital changes by remaining on track.

At long last, commend achievements and accomplishments en route to keep up with inspiration and force.

By following these means, an activity plan for execution can direct the fruitful execution of tasks and drives.

Tips for Staying on Track and Measuring Success

your prosperity, and gain persistent headway toward your objectives. Recollect that achievement is an excursion, and keeping focused is a continuous cycle.

Conclusion: The Power of a Simple, Effective Marketing Plan

All in all, the force of a basic, viable showcasing plan can't be undervalued. A very much-created promoting plan fills in as a guide for organizations, directing them towards their objectives and assisting them with interfacing with their "main" interest group in significant ways. By zeroing in on effortlessness and adequacy, organizations can augment their promoting endeavors and accomplish ideal outcomes.

A basic showcasing plan is clear, brief, and straightforward. It frames the objectives, main interest group, key informing, and methodologies for coming to and drawing in clients. By staying away from superfluous intricacy, organizations can impart their offer all the more successfully and guarantee that their advertising endeavors are firm and predictable.

Viability is the way to an effective showcasing plan. It expects organizations to distinguish and use the most significant promoting channels and strategies that resonate with their interest group. This might incorporate using online entertainment stages, content showcasing, email crusades, or conventional promoting strategies. By continually estimating and examining the aftereffects of their showcasing exercises, organizations can refine their procedures and advance their profit from speculation.

A basic, viable promoting plan enables organizations to settle on informed choices, distribute assets productively, and adjust to changing economic situations. It assists organizations with building brand mindfulness, producing leads, incrementing deals, and cultivating client steadfastness. In the present speedy and cutthroat business scene, a first-rate showcasing plan is fundamental for practical development and long-haul achievement.

In synopsis, the force of a straightforward, powerful promoting plan lies in its capacity to smooth out endeavors, boost effect, and drive business development. By putting time and assets into fostering an unmistakable and noteworthy showcasing plan, organizations can successfully explore the consistently developing promoting scene and accomplish their ideal results.

www.ingramcontent.com/pod-product-compliance
Lightning Source LLC
Chambersburg PA
CBHW070452220526
45466CB00004B/1802